The Little Boy Who Loved Dirt and Almost Became a Superslob

Story and Pictures by JUDITH VIGNA · Albert Whitman & Company, Chicago

Fourth Printing 1981

Text and Illustrations © 1975 by Judith Vigna

Published simultaneously in Canada by George J. McLeod, Limited, Toronto
All rights reserved.   Printed in U.S.A.

Library of Congress Cataloging in Publication Data

Vigna, Judith.
    The little boy who loved dirt and almost became a Superslob.

    SUMMARY: Jonathan James journeys in fantasy to the secret world of the Superslobs where washing is never necessary.

    [1. Hygiene—Fiction] I. Title.
PZ7.V67Li   [E]   74-14519
ISBN 0-8075-0865-9

The Little Boy Who Loved Dirt and Almost Became a Superslob

Jonathan **J**ames now and then
rolled in the mud
and splattered his food
and never hung his clothes,
except on trees.

Liking dirt, especially at bathtime, he dreamed of joining the Superslobs who, he'd heard, lived happily in **mud**.

And so he went
> (although he knew his mother wouldn't like it)
> to where...

...in deep dark tunnels, wearing mud

instead of clothes, the Superslobs lived.

They never washed and never brushed
and never bathed—and smelled.
And they ate dirt, mostly.

"You'll like it here, Jonathan James," they said. "You are quite the dirtiest little boy we've ever seen!"

And so he stayed (though sometimes thinking of his mother).

He rolled in the mud and splattered his food,
stuffed weeds in his ears, and was terribly rude.

His nails were growing disgustingly long,
and he never remembered
to flush the john.

He played bat-and-ball with rotten eggs,

and drew on the wall with greasy pegs.

And nobody said,

"That's dirty, Jonathan James, don't touch!"

Or, "Did you wash behind your ears?
Did you brush your teeth?"

Nobody bothered him at all.
That was the trouble,
    and he began to remember…

But the Superslobs said,
"You can't go home,
Jonathan James.
You are a Superslob,
and you belong with us."

"Wait," someone said.
"You can go home if
you pass our test.
If you are *not* a true Superslob
you can swim across the lake
to your home.
If you *are* a true Superslob, as soon
as you touch the water you will melt!"

Shivering and shaking, Jonathan James tiptoed in…

...then plunged,
and to his great surprise
did not melt.
In fact, it was rather nice,
warm and bright,
and felt good.

And when he reached the other side
and smelled his mother's hair,
it was nicer than dirt, even.

Introducing JUDITH VIGNA

Judith Vigna is English by birth, and her first professional training was at St. Martin's School of Art in London. When she came to the United States, she studied at the School of Visual Arts, Queens College, New York. In England, she used her skills as an artist and writer in public relations assignments, and in New York she did a stint as copywriter for the advertising agency of Young & Rubicam. Her concentration, however, moved away from this field as she began to work with emotionally disturbed children. Special courses in art therapy at Queens College have given her valuable insights in this new area.

Writing and illustrating were the only goals Judith Vigna recalls ever having. Beatrix Potter's little books enchanted her as a child, and Kenneth Grahame's animal friends were hers, too.

In her first picture book, *Gregory's Stitches,* Judith Vigna used humor and childlike exaggeration to help a youngster over a painful experience. Now in *The Little Boy Who Loved Dirt and Almost Became a Superslob* she enters into Jonathan James's fantasy of a secret world where washing's never necessary. But how reassuring it is that when the fantasy becomes too real, mother and home are warmly waiting.